DEAD

WIFE

WALKING

POEMS BY

JACQUELINE NEWMAN

A

THE AMAGANSETT PRESS

The author wishes to thank the editors of the following publications in which several of these poems first appeared: *American Jones*, *Bibliophilus*, *Into the Teeth of the Wind*, *Knightscapes*, *Out of Line*, *Poet Talk*, *Rockhurst Review*, *Rumps*, *Steamticket*, *Timber Creek Review*.

ISBN 0943959055
Library of Congress 2004 108741

© The Amagansett Press
Drawer 1070
Amagansett, NY 11930

Telephone:631-329-1151

Never say that marriage
has more of joy
than pain.

Euripides

PART ONE

TIIE WIFE

I bleed—
For your perversity—
These red words that make a stain
On your white washed claim that
She was out of line
And you were not to blame

Joni Mitchell

For:

The Mathematician Who Raised Me

The Man Who Knows Everything,
Except
The Location of Havameyer Street

The Two Most Magnificent
Works of Art Ever Created

Minnie

SIGN

Bought
to
hang
on a wall
that
has
not
been
lathed
in a house
that
has
not been built
this
photograph
colors
the
present
an
unexpected
sign
screams in silence
about
black
dawn
determination
truth
and
imagery.

DEAD WIFE WALKING

In her first book,
First chapter almost written
Boy meets girl.

Boy loves girl.
Girl loves boy.

Boy dumps her.
Girl cries.
He comes back
He wants to marry her
He spends the rest of his life cheating on her
She thinks they live happily ever after.

In her second book
Second chapter almost written
Boy meets girl

Boy loves boy
Girl loves boy

Boy tried to explain this to girl.
Girl cries.
Boy begs her to understand
He wants to marry her
She does not want to marry him
She is mad at him
She thinks he is an asshole
He still wants to marry her
He needs benefits for his partner
Eventually, after much fighting,
they marry
and live miserably ever after.

In her third book
(Hold to swallow handful of medication)
Third chapter almost written
Almost written because she is despondent
Boy meets girl

Boy pretends to love girl
Girl is obsessed with boy

Girl loves boy like she has never loved before
Boy only loves his MOTHER
Girl can't see this
His mother moves in
His mother starts cooking
His mother starts cleaning
She finally sees this
She tells him to take his mother to bed
(break to swallow more coffee and medication)
Only the mother lives happily ever after.

In her fourth book
Fourth chapter almost written
Boy meets girl

Girl tells boy to fuck off
Girl tells boy she is not interested

Girl is bitter
Girl is angry
Girl eats at the counter
Girl owns the remote control
Girl does what she wants when she wants
Girl pretends to live happily ever after.

In her fifth book
Fifth chapter almost written
Boy meets girl

Girl hallucinates
Girl hallucinates some more

She tells boy she loves him
Boy said I only asked for the time
Girl is confused
Boy is really orderly and takes the patient back to her
      room

For her sixth book
Sixth chapter almost written
Boy meets girl

Girl likes boy
Boy likes girl

Girl questions boy on the exact meaning of happily ever
      after
Boy falls in love with girl
Girl falls in love with boy
Girl truly believes she has found her soul mate
Boy gets girl pregnant and leaves her.

For her seventh book
Seventh chapter almost written
Boy meets girl
Girl hardly notices boy

She has her mind elsewhere
Girl ignores boy

She buys handgun
She shoots herself in the eye,
She shoots herself through the brain
No one lives happily ever after.

In her Eighth book
Eighth chapter almost written
Boy meets girl

Girl finds boy oddly attractive
Boy is hooked on girl

They have picnics in the orchard
They have showers in the moonlight
Girl falls in love with boy
Boy falls in love with girl
They have laughter under the boardwalk
Boy gets cancer and dies.

In her ninth book
Ninth chapter almost written
Boy meets girl

Girl has no strength to even look at boy
Girl just wants to crawl into a ball and die

Boy brings girl flowers
Boy brings girl sparkly rings
Boy brings an airplane professing his love
Girl is skeptical
Girl is afraid
Girl finally, finally relents
They marry and would have lived happily ever after
but Girl killed any feeling between them with her
constant obsessing and distrust of boy.

In her tenth book
Tenth chapter almost written
Boy meets girl

Girl winks at boy
Boy is shaken

Girl asks boy if he wants to go where it is more quiet
Boy checks for mace in his pocket
Girl is aggressive
Girl feels in control
Boy is suddenly attracted
Girl falls in love with boy
Boy falls in love with girl
They decide to move in together
It looks like they will live happily ever after
Author can not complete this chapter
as she is unable to provide an accurate description
of what living happily ever after means.
The publisher sends back the manuscript
and tells her to get a life.

BLOWING THE APOSTLE

Hated the cheery letters
you wrote,
hated the dog-breathed boy
and the mustached woman.
That circus clouded my vision.

>Such are constant memories,
>I want to be me again.

Hated the butchery way
you looked,
hated the way my heart broke
and life stuck up my ass.
That brutality stole my reason.

>This is past tense,
>I still want to be me again.

Hated the smarmy ambiance
you painted,
hated the whole gestalt
and the corner I was boxed into.
That theater of kindness broke me.

>This is finished,
>I am almost me again.

Hated the rosy artist
you wanted,
hated blowing the apostle
and the way he crawled home.
That was only the first cry for help.

>This is history,
>I am hoping to be me again, soon.

POEM TO A DREAM STEALER

Know this poem is for you
criminal dream stealer
homeless drug addict
son of a man who
taught you incorrectly.

Know this poem is for you
sponsored roofer
heartless launderer
son of a man who
taught you the rules.

Know this poem is for you
lonely wanderer
take take taker
son of a man who
taught you imprint.

Know this poem is for you
hirsute coward
bar-stool resident
son of a man who
taught you girls were bad.

Know this poem is for you
vanishing lover
cruel companion
son of a man who
taught a lifetime of ache.

OPEN FOR LIGHT

I am open for the miracle,
Will my hands bleed
Pool up and clog this day?
A Japanese girl
Smoking an American cigarette
Stepped down to extinguish the flame
But crushed a dead bird's skull instead.
When the blood and clear fluid
Made a puddle near the door
She cried.

There were no phone calls today.
Why spoil you?
That is what you would have said,
The master of bad timing
Or just a smart thing to say
When what you feel
Moistens your eyelashes
Pretending to be emotional
And frees you from feeling.

I am open for anything but the past
Which is forgettable
And does not keep me up
Night after night
Trying to put a sentence together
That is not a sentence
For either of us.
The silence of unspoken words is deafening.

A DICKENS NEIGHBORHOOD

New neighbors have moved in next door
to the mushroom house
where time really stopped.
They seem eager to meet
Victorian orphans,
and think you are the man of the house.

Their mouths open then stop.
You may offer up that you
are no one,
not interested,
someone who services this judge
with magnificent moon phases.

Like you, these new neighbors
steal food and services,
fattening to perfection.
This morning whines,
pockets are empty,
darkness will fill
all corners of the day.

Others before me know
nothing is as it appears anymore.
Tile cutters wet and wash what was.
Life propped up,
waxy in a window,
bitter, bitter, and old.

RECHARGED TO REFRAIN

The world sleeps recharged to refrain.

Awake eyes at 4:00
nightmares hound
mix of slamming car doors
nervous neighbors
who never, ever, ever
say hello.

The world sleeps recharged to refrain.

Do they have nightmares
that sparkle glint
blistering daylight
numbing words heated
corpse carried over shard pavement?

The world sleeps recharged to refrain.

Save this to document
before we lose
losing, always losing,
souls can't be held
won't stand still
such ache of night fall
in night play
where touch seems so incredibly real
and death just keeps on coming.

The world sleeps recharged to refrain.

CATCHING WHITE

If daylight could rearrange truth,
the fields of wheat
would grow fallow.
Empty loaves of bread speak to us as enemy,
hiding what infants they possess,
so as not to be bleached
or homogenized.

The stars know your secret is hate,
and the thought of you shining next to us
recoils firmament,
turning back gaseous skin
like a cosmic broken animal
poised for dietary slaughter.

In time you will ask
forgiveness
or want a check to blanket
the child left sleeping in a puddle of breast milk.
Humanity is forgotten
as your lips dance for the homeless,
to the tune of hard working mothers
who planted this land full of hungry children.

There will be no sky to balance
your vitriolic head wrap,
the irrational process,
as ignorance paints each generation heartless.
Starved for acceptance,
you run to a holy wordsmith,
who blesses you with sentence.
And white bread.

IMMOLATION IN FREE VERSE

You wanted
to quiet her.

Afraid she would
lecture you,
again,

you lit
her bed
on fire

Burning
her mouth
closed.

ATOMS IN A DREAM

He watched her
through darkness and leaves,
seasonally,
while she ate yogurt in the kitchen
late, every night.

They were both wearing
worn t-shirts,
only one of them
knew
he was there.

Climbing the tree outside the window,
compact bark itches.
He would wait,
nightly
with two hands
full of hard promise.

They would think:
atoms exist in dream making.

Each wished in moonlight.
She was cryptic
he waited for show.

He would sit
in the tree for hours.
She would pine
against an empty sink.

Wind on the back porch
swirled dead leaves,
dryly they would sing:

" There will always be someone to hurt
you."

THOUGHTS ELASTIC

Seasons teeter,
the sound of dying bugs
clogs the air,
colored with smells
of gardenias and fiery hair.

Shadow returns,
music mixed on
lined white paper,
pencil shavings
bring back what we always wanted.

Senses blur,
blues ache in folk music
books wait to be fingered
you become blue bird
flying in and out of mind's window.

September is almost here,
again, and again, and again
the same sameness wrinkles
time into complaint
then whines about loss.

Sir, why you?
What brews inside
snapping back thoughts elastic
when you have made it clear
there is no us that dances under any sky.

PORTRAIT

She's not like other girls.
Not this one.
This one breathes life into the dead.
Just like Jesus.

    She must know Jesus,
        because she mentions his name a lot.

She's not like other girls.
Not this one.
This one swings a hammer and fixes anything
    broken.
Just like Daddy.

    She must not know Daddy,
        because she rarely mentions his name at all.

MOTHER

It was you breezing in and out like a tropical storm flaunting its balmy perfume. Forever a changing forecast of variable behavior, your slowly brewing storm-front a thunderclap of words. Neighborhood barometers held you up as unstable, a bi-polar twist of face. You set your children adrift in a squall of humanity and let them drown in the rain of your hands. No one could predict the highs or lows stormy Mother. Your children grew mercurial, raising themselves from the air, with no radar to guide them. No tracking system to bring them home.

PERMISSION

An Bhuil Cead Agaim Dull Amach

Why do I ask when I am full grown?
Sweeping cinders from
nothing to nowhere,
on this predictable hideous road
seeking permission
to breathe.

An Bhuil Cead Agaim Dull Amach

Who grants me permission to fly?
Climbing weekdays as rocky hills,
seeking foothold,
bloodied knees,
seconds from landslide,
high enough to see
puddles of what's wrong.

An Bhuil Cead Agaim Dull Amach

What will save me from this cruel stepmother?
Locked up, twisted tight,
caged within your house
barbed wire tongue
squeezing every drop of life
from your subservient subject.

UNCOVERED DISTRACTION

It was the baseball season.
That year dragged on and on,
through snow, heat wave, wind
and endless, ceaseless, demanding rain.
That season, night after night
tucked in with TV, thoughts meandered inward.

It was the baseball season
and distraction was up at bat.

That distraction turned the seasons quiet
leaves fell onto snow, melting onto buds in time,
after frost, pitchers and catchers day,
summer distraction was uncovered.
The sticky air stuck arms to armchairs,
runners fell on their faces,
bench warmers prayed to get some action.
Who knew then that as snowflakes would fall,
we would be back where we started:
on the injured list, with no souvenirs.

It was the baseball season
and cold hearted bastards were up at bat.

Now we seed the green square diamond
planting magic and earnest honesty,
this will be our championship season.
Focused on focusing, we have a job to do,
ghosts whisper to distract.
We have come to play, come to glue back our hearts,
a foul life is not orbital,
we can't be thrown into a nameless crowd.

It was the baseball season
and freedom was up at bat.

RAINLESS SUMMER

It's summer now.
Much work looms ahead,
beneath and beyond.
Piles of piles near the
nonexistent shed,
for which there are plans,
piled somewhere in the piles.

There are plans, and piles and lists.
That is who I have become.
I am a pile, a plan and a list.

This summer has seen no rain.
The sun beckons me to
celebrate daylight and fragrance,
salt and sea air.

The lists pile higher,
plans gain dust and ash,
my skin darkens
as this earth cracks and dries.

It is your time now.
Then, there were rainy days
and plans were soon unlisted.
Piles were poems I wrote about you.

No rain saves face,
our insides know.
I dreamt of bunnies last night.
Dreams are hurtful.

They lounge in the brain
like summer heat.
You stick to my
heart like vinyl.

THE DEATH OF INFINITE POSSIBILITY

Wrong!
Good night old man.
I'm turning the light out,
my mind off,
the vacuum on.

Your truth pulled down with a tug
what soared as imagination.
The useless gather from an empty well,
such are the masses with which I mingle.

Wrong!
Good night old man.
The thin ledge of hair
you wear in front
makes me want to jump suicidal.

Untold depths of unrequited tenderness
dried up on this tongue.
The death of infinite possibility
buried this immediate corpse
in yet another grave of infidelity.

Wrong!
Good night old man.
You could have fevered subcutaneous,
or sweetened the moment,
instead the uneasy sweat salted my wounds.

ASYLUM DUET

Sitting by the window, in spite of reason, he asked
for three wishes.
With a starched smile, and stark white impatience,
she agreed to grant them.

He asked for fire.

    She gave fire to him as dance.
    With warmth, she moved lightly
    On his forehead, disarming him.

        He ate the footsteps,
        spewing back orange-blue words
        that burned a hole through the earth.

He asked for rain.

    She gave rain to him as song.
    With rhythm, she hummed softly
    In his ear, disarming him.

        He listened as each drop fell on
        gurgling excuses without boundaries,
        drowning the obvious in hopelessness.

He asked for moonlight.

    She gave moonlight to him as medication.
    With prayer she washed chalky pills
    Down his throat, disarming him.

        He swallowed thoughtlessly,
        barking out jagged moonbeams
        that littered this ward.

IRONICALLY IRONIC

The irony was that
he kept saying
things were "ironical,"
so ironic.

There's no getting
to California,
even cold north California.
Now,
trying to keep weekend warm,
Saturday night tea, inside,
no need to drive, to freeze.
That is freedom.
The freedom is for doing nothing.

"Ironical," he would say
so ironic.
He could be so wrong.

In 1977 the drive across state lines
kept esteem down,
lost people wept all the way to the vineyard,
with cream cheese
and caviar melting in the crush.

There were no dimes in their pockets
the poetry then seemed confessional, ironic,
wordsmiths got handouts
rhyme dealt them bed and board,
pretty ones slept with sand and sea.

"It was incredibly ironical," someone said.
So ironic.

I thought of him, I thought of me.
One of us was always wrong.

LOOKING FOR HAVAMEYER STREET

It always started out badly
this family joke
a euphemism for directions,
unfolding maps into
a thick skin that shriveled over time
into that which remained unspeakable.

This surely could not be Mercy Street
though the neighborhood does look familiar
dressed in a twisted pink of brain and green.
Here the murky demons differ,
churning against tide, title and time,
they stay without,
no one is here to let them in.

Who might mistake this ride as comfort?
Bumpy word filled seasons crash
then collide into tender tin,
gold leafed years heaped like junk
near the rats and remnants of life.

Draw a line down this back seat
segregating what's good from such evil,
searching for something unreachable
in the darkened depths of blue dusk
where spirits pump you full of yourself
you still stand alone
still looking for Havameyer Street
waiting to find direction.

THE BEAUTY OF NOTHING

Fell back, lost the breadcrumb highway
Derailed out-of-town
On unfamiliar secrets
First time for nothing
Nothing sparkled more
Nothing was no longer something.

Tripped up, forgot the map
Took unwheeled baggage
Looking for treasure
Visa denied
Nothing needs to be altered
The seams have unraveled themselves.

Confused by flash and flower
Went on a tourist vacation
Drinking icy hotel liquor
Until night's finger poked the sandman
To commemorate reality
A final swallow before crossing the red line.

Uncovering tracks to define rut
Stiff soldier dolls point out groove
Impaled carousel horses glide up and down
Direction knows it's back and forth
Direction is clear when nothing beckons
Nothing no longer holds any interest.

SEASONED DREAMER

In the dream there was yellow.
Blinding yellow that gave
the Catholic girl's school
a halo, and walked a black cat
across the street to the waiting
pink Cadillac, top down,
secular and anticipatory.

In your basement,
a middle aged woman
crawled through a bed sheet,
vertically hung,
boxing off your life
from the next chapter.

Strange figures held back packs taut, backwards
against their flannel-plaided chests.
Your wife was surprised to meet me,
Though she was sure I belonged
to the giants, and slithered with other men.

Last night, the arms of the maroon wool jacket
closed tight, like an asthmatic's lung,
while we waited in a museum's gift shop,
where stained glass religion hung high and
intimidated.
Angels whispered the word absurd,
and we found ourselves unsure of what to do.

We looked for a book of answers,
without questions, the letters became random,
painting nonsensical patterns
that looked like dead women wearing scarves.
These women sang hymnally:
"broken glass and water are very good signs in
                                        dreams."

RESERVOIR POEM

It's over.
Over on such beautiful a day
with magnificent attention
to spring's lush bounty,
jittery blue lake,
random parking lot.

The only thing more than over
was over and left to lose, years ago
in a basement, a dirty basement
ticked mattress, urine reservoir.

It's over, the witch had her day
all pumpkins are evil
the devil wears jeans.

Again, it's over.
All that is left
is a fuzzy wingless bee.
The buzz buzz of whisper says:
"glass slippers
can be used to slit wrists."

It's over. Give it up.
Hidden tears,
howling cries penetrate nothing.
For nothing is all that stands
in the space where nothing was
when over is at an end.

Move on - move on - move on - move on.
Somewhere is an upstate castle,
with jagged green pines
it hides a slate underbelly
with direct view of a reservoir.

It is serious now.
It is over.
It is not.

PART TWO

THE POET

Poetry is not a turning loose of emotion,
but an escape from emotion;
it is not the expression of personality,
but an escape from personality.
But, of course,
only those who have personality and emotions
know what it means to want to escape from these
things.

T.S. Eliot

AT LUNCH WITH THE POET LAUREATE

He didn't really ask me. I asked him.
Well, I pushed myself in front of the autograph
        hounds,
literary groupies and disabled English teachers.
I was trying to impress him with my grooviness.
Nothing I do works. Ever.

This time it was different. I sweat desperation.
I should know by now. I wanted a poetic lunch.
Time to talk about me.
So I elbowed my way in front of:
elderly book worms, middle-aged first-edition-with-
        an-autograph-owners,
and the aforementioned disabled English teachers.

Boldly I said: "Hey…uh listen…uh…do you want to
        have lunch with me?"
And he said: "Who are you?"
I stammered most gracefully, I waved at the crowd
        behind me,
my eyes drifting over the wheelchairs,
I looked back at him most empathetically,
"Oh kind sir, I am with these fine folk!"

I lied. I lied big.
And I used disabled strangers to get a lunch date
        with the poet laureate.
He asked if it was for us alone, or with my group.
I explained that in a week or so, I would no longer
        be in charge
of such a large domain. I explained that in a week or
        so,
I would be in charge of my senses.
I asked him to lunch. And he said yes.
So we spoke of poetry,
and I spit out quotes and phrases until his eyes
        glazed over.

Over.

And this reminded me of one English II class that I
    adored.

We had read this man's poetry for days and weeks
    and days.

We had been given an audience with the Pope of
    Poetry

and we were just about to meet him.

I asked the class what they would be interested in
    hearing most.

The voice came from the front row and then the
    back:

"We want to know how he combs his hair from one
    side to the other?"

"What happens when he takes a shower?"

So I watched the poet laureate eat lettuce
    overpowered by blue cheese

and I wondered if I should tell him this story, or find
    out for myself.

Myself is me. And it's always about me.

Even when it's not about me I find a way to turn it
    into something about me.

I told him this story.

He blushed when I got to the part about the shower.

The afternoon wound down with the appropriate
    shadow references

coloring the back wall and mood.

My tongue became stronger, I commented on the
    beauty of the day.

If no one stopped me, would I talk about myself
    forever?

I wondered if that is why there are other people out
    there.

Protection from ourselves.

I wanted him to ask me to go fishing.
Right there I had a vision.
We could go fishing in his toilet right before
we stepped into the shower.
My humor clearly began to annoy him.

Lunch ended there.
I would not come back armed
with the secret of comb-overs
or what one might catch
from a toilet.

THE DAY I MET LEWIS CARROLL

Yesterday, I met a man who really, really believed
    he was Lewis Carroll.
He announced quite operatically, for all who would
    listen,
that he had come in early, specifically to see the
    doctor.
Urgently he stammered, "I have an emergency
    appointment!"
Taking out an imaginary date book, he pointed to his
    blank palm, and exclaimed:
"I am Lewis Carroll, the very famous author and
    mathematician!"
He looked very homeless, crunched up and
    wrinkled, like a used take-out bag.

There was no doctor to see him; we were in a
    bookstore.
The bookstore manager, who had been briefed,
    greeted Lewis Carroll.
Briefed, but not particularly patient,
he was tired of throwing out drunken yarn spinners
    and intellectual shoplifters.
The manager coughed authoritatively, and in his
    most sarcastic snip,
let Mr. Carroll know that Dr. Seuss was not taking
    on any new patients at this time.

Clearly that was a brilliant move and should have
    worked immediately,
but all those who had witnessed the entertainment
    started to laugh and clap.
Lewis Carroll was hip; he was waiting for his close-
    up:
" I have an appointment to see the doctor!"
What a close-up it was, his teeth numbered only
    seven and had grown long,

his shirt and pants were both orange, striped, and
    solid.
Nothing really matched, but after such a crisis, they
    started to work for me.

Between seconds and choice of movement there is
    much time.
Lewis Carroll saw everyone staring at him; he
    bathed only in this attention.
To distract us, to refocus the moment, he smiled and
    wet his pants.
Urine started to pool on the carpet, rolling towards a
    stack of romance novels.
A bearded grad student yelled out: "Whoa buddy,
    that really stinks!"
Lewis Carroll started to vent fully: "Well, certainly
    now you see why I need a Doctor!" Cash
    registers refused to ring, no one moved.

Life as a floorshow is swallowed daily, two
    uniformed police officers arrived
laughing, at first they pretended they were
    customers, only there to buy books.
Mr. Carroll was finally subdued while making
    invisible margin notes in no book.
I stood stunned on a rug soaked with infected urine.
An old lady with rouge circles, spackled in make-up
    muttered to herself:
"I wonder why more people don't pee in public for
    attention?"

NORTHEAST MELT

Poets congregate there
protected by bedrock breasts
velvety lichen
looking for spirits
in glass or moss.
Liquid reminders
that life can be
summed up with mountains.

Poets tend to attach themselves
to roots that grow in cracks
upstate, where mountains eat sky
while adverbless strangers
tie a trailer to this pity.

Poets will refuse to see you
underneath their words
the raw nerves become
songs that just play on
and on and on and on and on.

Poets give up,
give back,
give up again.
Checking body bags
hiding organs in caves
sliding vowels into genetics.

Poets follow form,
fixing empty offers
that offer emptiness
to any artist who bleeds.

DESK CLERK IN A BERGEN COUNTY MUSEUM

I think that it should be
me splayed against these walls,
white flatlands home to someone else's
mute colored slices of life.
My talent seems to elude me,
I've never even come close,
the ladder I won came without rungs.

I should have stayed in my crib,
comfortable in my feces,
raging and wet,
without focus or family.
I can't even make fire from fire.

I hand out maps and stamp hand backs.
Inside me there is something.
I believe in me.
Thinking I'm there, thinking I'm right there,
I forget what I'm doing, I get distracted.

Now I sit with wasted time bunched up my ass.
Staring at these walls all day, my insides become
        electric,
I pretend to be a painting of a naked woman,
sometimes I get to where I want to touch myself.

Life ties me down with shredded veins of human
        canvas.
And I am left to sit here,
perpendicular to the Masters,
stamping hand backs and handing out maps.

NOUNS

Before one o'clock this day
I fell into another trance
without the river flowing backwards.
Unsure of every person, place, or thing.
Trust no nouns is what I think.

I was out.
I was really deep in noun thought,
partially clothed, partially closed,
lost in the same thought:
just a noun, a proper noun.

Questions about questions about questions
sparked more thought.
Copernicus comes around a lot and other heretics
    abound,
shame is being smashed,
and the trance should teach.
And the nouns move on.

There was climax then trance,
blue forgiveness, ocean water crashing.
I am there. I am really there.
Nouns can feel other nouns.

I became aware of the trance through my hands.
The ones without fingerprints,
working hands, forging words like this,
noun words,
noun thoughts of nouns to propel me.

CRUMBS OF YOU

There was her name:
Vivian.
Not even spelled the right way,
the romantic way, the way Tom liked it.

There was proof:
Vivian.
That night, your drawers were emptied
as you slept alone,
letters were read in an attempt to know you.

There was no:
Vivian
then.
Only midnight car rides
on unknown islands littered with
data entry cards, pot smoke, and youth.

There it is:
Vivian.
She does not know
what could have happened,
Thanksgiving when cramps turned
an un-vacation into unemployment.

There, I said it:
Vivian.
She must be lonely,
crying out for more then you give her.
She feels sorry for herself,
the blank stare reaches out to past lovers,
the arms that never hugged.

There is no sorrow for:
Vivian.
I am cruel in my want of you,
and will take whatever tattered thread is worn,
any crumb of you
should be swept into my mouth.

SELF PORTRAIT #16

She licks at every
opportunity,
literate and guttural.
She is licked.
Oh, she knows it is over.

         (This is why it is called portrait.)

Again and again, she knows there is no chance
of irrigating a desert
with vowels,
or nourishing the southern coastline
with self-absorption.

         (This is why it is called portrait.)

The last time she drank prose,
her career spilled out,
splashing her smug soaked self
everywhere.
She puddled,
offending the tenured help.

         (This is why it is called portrait.)

Someone should warn her,
give her what she wants,
a subject-verb agreement,
a secret within a secret,
something no one else has.

         (This is why it is called portrait.)

She dances in vocabulary,
perfumed word drops,
writing in the car with
another life-raft full of dreamers.

BLACKENED WAND

It was time to give up the magic wand,
the twig,
the stick that makes whole.
Was time.
Was done.

Wishes are feeble myths
for the non-religious,
the disbelievers that pray.
Was finished.
Was done.

Replicators replicating inchoate
for the unable,
willingness seeps into timelessness.
Was wanted.
Was done.

The dolls were classified
scattered stuffing
working cloth tongue.
Was actualized.
Was done.

Not trying to be Edith with words
writing mornings in manor
with action towards beauty.
Was thought.
Was done.

No one reads what has been written
dripped out of glittery blackened castles
magic wands meter out next moves.
Was childish.
Was done.

SONG TO A MILITANT POET

His words march
to the right-handed beat
of a fleshy metronome.
Painted and wired,
plugged into a confused generation
of software, baby's daddies and
women who bleed imagery for attention.
These eyes sense a scientific Medusa,
personal issues that whirl
for a dervish called diary.

       When we were you, we kept it secret.

The walls he built are transparently opaque.
Evolution means to unfold,
not mutate.
Silence moves off his tongue,
his words break up with linguistic static.
The moon you covet is ours,
light can not be shielded by barbed wire.
We know this game,
lost pieces have been replaced
with rock and designer wear.
There is no magic to a word like fuck.

       When we were you, we kept it secret.

Nature's haiku is syllabic,
it's been written and rewritten.
Your every word has worn thin,
threadbare poetry
that flashes of monkeys
at the keyboards.
To dribble with the big boys
you've got to rework this act.
If you take it on the street too soon
you risk being road kill.

       When we were you, we kept it secret.

WE CIRCLE. WE CYCLE.

Wonderfully black,
shadowless, wet,
seagull songs are painfully Semitic,
each laughing caw
points to suffering,
weathervane bow,
a pocket violin.

Salty branches drip tears,
pockmarked swollen puddles,
circle in circles,
swiftly moving workmen
rush past swiftly,
their under eye circles repeat
this concentric pattern,
over and over we circle.
We cycle.

Today was yesterday,
and somewhere, tomorrow,
again and again and again.
The skin we wear should fit,
we tried it on,
it should belong to us.
We are stretched,
unfamiliar,
unfulfilled,
unaware,
unhappy underneath
what thoughts we carry around
in circles
when we cycle,
in silence, in dreams.

BLACK-EYED OPUS

Upstate, where black eyes swim away
from a drive-by commitment,
writer's hands pencil my breasts
in a silent park umbrellaed by traveling salesman
stars.
Desperate desire intensifies how quickly
human love decays.

Upstate, where a face-to-face kiss
stands shoulder to shoulder against a
black-eyed khaki stick shift, held until
purring machinery is forsaken or taken for granted.
This tender animal will never be put back together
this moment came without directions
frightening foreign language agendas
into a jumbled pile of extra screws.

Upstate, where a black-eyed dream of symmetrical
fences
penned in academic poets that confessed bold
intensity
institutionalized professors twitched in tweed
in front of disinterested audiences bearing falsified
blood lines.
No ticket home will ever heal the shame of wanting
to
lick moonlight off your belly.

Upstate, where poetic whispers curdle in your arms
heartless tongues paint a sentence of indifference
years of ignorant blind faith killed the fragile
gardener
who planted cerebral roots in an unfamiliar
cottage where she had signed on to
taste the softest kisses but was poisoned
by black-eyed prose and snake oil.

MAYBE

He takes care
of what needs to be taken care of
and what doesn't.

He runs from storm surged ocean water
scared of the waves
unbalanced future.

He speaks thought in many colors
words that arc with the sun
and fall shy of the truth.

He is ready for the sentence
a distant want to create stanza
miserable empty rooms litter the years.

He walks with ease akimbo
talking to the dollies
lecturing on normalcy.

He wants to empty the sandbox
and fill it with seed
then nourish the garden he planted.

TRAIN STATION IN IPSWICH

Nature poems flash metaphorically
in dreams of Ipswich,
where the Beach People congregate.
They live in humid tents,
eat whole fried soft-shelled crabs
and have built a crowded city
out of discarded seashells.

There were directional signs
that read: upstate New York,
near the shiny one: Florida, one mile.
Each was splattered yellow,
hanging high between
food canteen and train station,
over the heads of overloaded vacation seekers.

The Beach People were
Steinbeckian, muddy, empty gazed,
at first welcoming
then deadly as drunken beach blonds
tattooed and terrifying
with fingernails so dirty they smelled.

Some found the crab people disturbing,
coloring hours and days with certainty.
The retelling of left-right issues,
pretending to really understand Ginsberg.
Grey-haired women wore rainbow scarves,
their shells hard under
the transparent breeding.

Some want to be what Beach People eat,
for in analogous Ipswich,
dreams taste of want.

ON WRITING A NATURE POEM IN LATIN

Born that Thursday,
ending a month-long solstice,

cars balanced on a fault line.
No longer were parts created whole.

Dead words in Latin mock this creator.

Sun shadows late summer branches,
no one notices.

Smoke and age paint the pine board,
future wood rot dressed as wet leaf underbrush.

The cycle feeds upon itself.

Hairless men, waxed heartbreak,
acceptance cloaks renewal.
There is only one poem in each of us.

We spend lifetimes putting new words in
old spaces.

SILENCE HAS NOWHERE TO SING

Sometimes
she wants to talk
in purple streaks,
planting words in the air
that will never take root
and most misunderstand.

There is much jazz
in her speech,
minor key misfit,
dissonant sound between
chord and key.

Errors of the heart
the head
burn in a hidden pipe.
She smokes away the present,
someone could have
saved her.

She makes use of tense,
hanging phrase as art,
anxious canvas,
one stroke away from stroke.

Silence has nowhere to sing
when ethnic newcomers import
bad rhyme or watery tea.
She always knew
the road home
was badly out of sync.

PARAGRAPH

Word
edges
fit.

Dovetailed
lifetime
of

beauty
in
sentence.

Letters
take
breath.

They
inflate
sound

to
say
ahhhhhhhhh.

PRIZE

She started to compose
Some letter
Some thought
Some composure to her composition.

She started to think
Some words
Some feelings
Some thought to her thoughts.

She tried to stay woven
Some warp
Some tapestry
Some ravel to her unraveling.

She tried to understand
Some silence
Some sign
Some pennies she found in the park

She tried to move on
Some purpose
Some meaning
Some curtain that would fall.

PART THREE

THE GEOGRAPHY OF WORDS

It's not true that life is
one damn thing after another;
it is one damn thing over and over.

Edna St. Vincent Millay

CITY LIFE

We
are
glass
truth:
caged.

Anger
is
always
the
same
dead
claw.

I
bark
and
howl
on
edge.

Scratching
change
from
the
sky.

I SEEK TO BE RURAL

I was urban.
Now I am suburban.
I seek to be rural.

          I was long.
          Now I am spiked.
          I seek to retain it.

I was battered.
Now I am dipped.
I seek to fry.

          I was dreaming.
          Now I am focused.
          I seek to know.

I was magic.
Now I am aged.
I seek to laugh.

          I was angry.
          Now I am numb.
          I seek to be rural.

URBAN SELF PORTRAIT

I was born there:
in the canyons of cement
ankle-deep in tickertape,
where the asphalt coughs steam
and sidewalks glisten
like a diamond sandwich.

I grew tall there:
on broken bottle playgrounds,
kicking glass
and dog-shit past
glue-sniffers and baby carriages,
pretending to be an orphan.

I found work there:
in paste-faced human rivers
that churned into each other mosaic,
crumbling the self
until who you are
is what you do.

I ran away from there:
packed my womb,
foregoing breadcrumbs.
This new skin wears a rake,
gathering empty plates of time.

PEACE SHADOW

She was in and out of dreams today,
by the dead-fish river,
smelling ocean tide people and fantasy.
She was somewhere else,
her head filled with conversation
guardian mouths were empty,
he wanted to say not you
and love me
and you're a baby.

Her place is empty today,
a warm rain frizzles
yellow leaves line the stairs,
nature's linoleum.
She walked here, saw no one, never anyone to see,
just Soho restaurant ceiling patterns
In the dead-fish river
where she waited for nothing
and everyone.

Confused geese lined up near her feet
they smiled, they wanted to be swans,
like her.
In shadow everyone wants something,
or someone
or to be something else.
The silent, empty dead fish river was neither low nor high.
It was just tide rushing, memory, relation.
She stood there lost. . . somewhere else
dressed in thoughts of earlier within earshot of a silent river.

Wet blacktop screech is melodic today.
Rushing cars on wet pavement sound like rushing water, silently.
She is back home, about to go out again
might smoke in the commons where peace reigns.
An oily film covers and smudges,
she hides her words.
Thoughts firm in fact:
When she says never
it never means you.

ABOVE

He sits on his jagged granite mountain
and wants to take someone home
to shine memory.
There is sunset begging
for treeline attention.

               Lakes lay low in wait of want.

He sits on his rounded green briar mountain
and wants to celluloid people watch
for stolen hearts.
Wishes are wind chimes for the feeble,
summer cement hardens, flesh grows cold.

             Binary messages flash left flash right.

He sits on his petrified cliff
and wants what is not offered
using loaded words to shoot a star.
The victim draws his own chalk outline
digs a respectable grave.

             Fights to accept an unbearable skin.

He sits on his craggy bluff
and brings music that wears out welcomes
similar similarities as ocean tide breathes.
Affectations abound with sea glass
alcohol disinfects a lack of horizon.

             The finish line demands photographic evidence.

ATLANTIC CITY

Seedy ghetto
The aged poor
Tethered to slot machines
Pumpkin lovers
Sea glass crowns
Broken neon

Plastic, plastic, plastic.

Like old Vietnam
Throwing dice
Needles, shells, and condoms
Ghostly shadows
Empty Ferris wheel
Rusty engineering
Clowny music
Aviary footprints
Treated boardwalk

Plastic, plastic, plastic.

Crack whores
Pawn lives
Opulent wildflowers
Photograph the dead
Buildings missing teeth
Blue burgers
Red pens

Plastic, plastic, plastic.

THE DAY SCRUFFY BECAME A SPEED BUMP

Pedro had just moved all of his belongings
to the dry earth, underneath a rusted semi
that was missing some wheels over on Jefferson Street.
The grass grew wild with ticks and old tires.
They called this squalor their summer residence, a place where
man and beast could laugh together in such a humid swamp as
    summer.

Wherever Pedro stood, Scruffy would shake beside him,
starving the fleas that tried to make a home in flesh.
They called him "Wonder Dog!"
Neighborhood status came from this canine miracle:
the ability to locate Pedro all over town, anywhere he might be.
Drinking men would toast Scruffy, brown bags in hand:
"If my wife found me like this dog does you, I'd shoot myself!"
"Or her." They would all laugh mid-sentence,
spitting beer and happy saliva on anyone that was listening.

Deaf and missing one leg, Scruffy could actually smile.
He had five more teeth than Pedro.
This kind of love was unbeatable, unbendable,
unbreakable as cobblestone embedded in the street,
which is where George happened onto him,
running over Scruffy with his truck,
going ba-rump, ba-rump.

Pedro saw it all from beginning to end, slow motion,
from his chair under the only peach tree in Hoboken.
Pedro started to cry, muffled howls at first,
twisting his sneaker rubber into the dirt, making circles,
until after a while he pretended not to care.
He pretended to kick ticks off the grass.

George won't buy Pedro a new dog, or say "I'm sorry."
He says everyone knows Pedro can't afford to feed himself,
let alone a hungry, flea-ridden dog.
Late at night, underneath the rusty truck on Jefferson Street.
Pedro can't sleep anymore, he misses Scruffy's breathing.
The only sound he hears now is ba-rump, ba-rump.

SNIFF WIRE

Not shooting-up now only because the storm outside is threatening to get worse and driving high is too hard. Too wired at times to talk, slurring words and tonguing cheek until the first layer of skin roughs off. You and your friends are laughing on the wire..... sniffing lines right down the middle of the street. The car is coming around the curve, in the place where you can't see or hear it. It speeds towards you as you suck up stomped on crystals . Your diarrhea comes from Italy…your laughter through Florida.

Not shooting-up now only because the storm outside is threatening to get worse and driving high is really very hard. Too wired at times to swallow, spitting creamy saliva into napkin after napkin after napkin. You and your friends are laughing in New Jersey sniffing lines right down the middle of the street. The car is getting closer…prayers are said to see you crushed…to see you fail. Someone jokes your face should kiss the windshield. Everyone wished to see you die. Laughter runs down the back of your throat.

Not shooting-up now only because the storm outside is threatening to get worse and driving high is impossible when the dealer does not call. Too wired at times to sit still, cowering in the corner behind a locked door held shut by three locks and a desk. You and your friends are laughing outside a stranger's house, sniffing lines right down the middle of the street. Careless frat boys playing chicken, hiding behind a locked door, using religion as a euphemism for fucking an old girlfriend. The car slams you hard and hits you in the head first. Silence looms after broken glass. Smug laughter weighs a full bag.

ARCHANGEL ON TENTH STREET

She started thinking about rank the night the thunderstorm
      came in.
Town fathers were milling about, accepting their lives in
      denial,
feeling a need to wash themselves in God,
when his messenger arrived in a beat-up Buick.
You could feel his care:
      "Love with wheels is still love."

Revival tents filled with sweat and perfume
bonded the neighborhood here, fanning themselves,
      waiting to surrender.
She was thinking about Jesus and was trying
to fall to her knees convincingly. She wanted to be whole.
And fed.
You could feel his care:
      "Love with nothing tangible is still love."

That summer, our man in the Skylark,
wearing a tie in the land of T-shirts and trailers,
willed us to be faithful.
knowing the air to be thick and molecular,
painting us nightfall, we surely tried believing.
Proving our devotion by parting of beer and lipstick
      dollars.
You could feel his care:
      "Love with loss is still love."

She needs flesh and bone.
He wants it hard and real.
Under the tent bleachers, where hymn pages
wrinkled in the rain, she watched her sins wash away upon
      this southern earth.
Soaked in his stare, another weekend baptismal,
jumping into the fire, they are joined by neighbor and
      child,
intent on buying God, repenting on a bi-monthly basis.
She knelt in the rain, as thunder shook the tent and trees,
watching him watch her redemption.
Dry in the back of his Buick,
she could feel his care:
      "Love without feeling is still love.

PART FOUR

THE TRIBE

Not everything that can be counted
counts,
and not everything that counts
can be counted.

Albert Einstein

TRIBE

The elders stood in a circle
upright, righteous, devout.
back light shadowed them colored:
dusty smoke, clay red, smudged gray.

Their voices sounded garbled through the fabric
             of the tent,
we listened with primal ears.
Our sun walks in line, shadows sleep,
voices became less random,
masculine and throaty, tied to birthright.

At their feet, bloodied in battle,
a buffalo,
out of breath, steamy,
wet and heavy like a bathroom rug.
Death trickled out his triangle nose.
The elders constantly changed position,
pointing up,
pointing down.
From above it looks like cave painting,
ancient in need,
older than hunger.

Grandpa left the circle, whispering in our tent,
on his knees, searching for what seemed like
             noise.
He came back to the circle,
unwrapping tissue paper from the continent,
presenting the finest in airport cutlery.
They carved dinner and clothing for twelve.
Aunts came crying for entrails,
children took teeth to make dice.

The full moon hushed us.
Tomorrow we salt the bloodied muscle,
pounding out all water,
or any other trace left of life.

BRYNDAL

No one calls.
They called her Bryndal.
Pushed out feverishly,
to one named at birth
by two selfish lovers.

Named and then forgotten.
Words pinned to her chest,
left naked, distant voyager,
over walls and through them.

No one calls.
Or calls her home.
She is Bryndal,
goddess of nothing to say.
We are just words.

We tend to offend strangers
with seminal desire.
Beaten daily, professionally,
with closed fists,
this hand she has been dealt,
worn as lisp, cloaked in heavy shame,
laying down her flesh as sword.

No one calls.
Calling out colors
in the aging present,
weathered sunset skin,
She dances in the blue loss of lost,
hidden treasure, trunk full of lies.
The unfaithful leap,
welts go,
memories stay.

THE CONFESSION

I shot my daughter through the head.

This frustrated, angry policeman,
spewing spit-mist between fattened purple lips,

told me to repeat the story.
Again.

It's like I told you:
I shot my daughter through the head.

I didn't mean to do it.
Not really.

Not at first.
It was getting near Christmas,

and I just can't afford stuff she don't need.
That hypno-light of boxed TV sang to her.

It convinced her my love depended on it.
She told me she knew that I would never let her down.

I shot my daughter through the head.
Now she won't be disappointed for Christmas.

THE LIST OF THE TORTURED UNHOLY

There was the day it began
no one named Elvis left the building
no one left the building at all
tear gas smashed down gates
with rifle packing teenagers.

There was only that day
we all were list-makers, list-livers
on the List of Tortured Unholy.
Some never got up,
Some never got away.

There was that day
when heaven and hell
held us between tweezers
threatening to drop us off in big cities,
or worse, bring us home.

There was that day that could have been that day
when the multi-ethnic multi-tasked
wanted to be King.
Every person wore
gold sunglasses and black sideburns.
We should have been disabled lesbian Elvis
impersonators,
but we all were the same.
All were strangers, grouped to die,
naked and trembling, poor and forgotten.

So on that day,
instead of jumping into a jumpsuit,
or jumping off the roof
we tried bridging the opposites,
we tried to ward off delusions
held together by belief.
I am Fat Elvis, the tortured unholy,
but I hung on.

WHEN MOTHER WAS GONE

I would drown your hands
in a shark tank
so they could not touch
anymore innocent breasts
in darkened places
when mother was not at home.

I would take your hands
apart muscle by cell
so their dexterity
could no longer clamp nipples
between forefinger and thumb
when mother was away from her post.

I would smash your hands
into piles of dust
so they could not feel
memories of baby's skin
and hidden meanings
when mother would leave for no reason.

I would drown your hands
in a shark tank, old Uncle
but I have just heard
you finally passed away.

ST. LUCY

He taught blind boys
to have sex.
Convinced unsteady mothers
to relinquish their giggly sons
for medicinal value.

He taught blind boys
to stroke their raging manhood
without benefit of
visual stimulants
or female interaction.
The mothers chain smoked
outside the unlocked door.

He taught blind boys
to surrender openly,
circled naked campers.
Symmetrical erections
point to the one thing
mother can't teach them.

He taught blind boys
to find focus.
They pleasured themselves
and each other until the day
grew faint and crepuscular.
Exploding for science,
the boys smiled,
while the mothers pretended
to look satisfied.

HATE AND WARM SPIT

The crowd screamed: "Burn It!"
                    they yelled into the air
                    filling empty spaces with
                    hate and warm spit.

All manner of recall:
                    green football jerseys
                    opaque sea-glass, Daddy's shells
                    hate and warm spit.

The crowd screamed louder: "Burn It!"

                    they demanded a cleansing fire
                    dragon's breath drools while dragging
                    hate and warm spit.

All manner of recall:
                    Christian nightstand bibles
                    sportsmen fanfare
                    hate and warm spit.

The crowd screamed loudest: "Burn It!"

                    Full moon shines on those who use women
                    shame follows anal retention
                    embers glow on hate and warm spit.

ANOTHER RIVER THOUGHT

Storm swept branch twiglet
looked wormy, wet and pink,
did not squiggle or slither
on the uneven brick,
round from wear and weather.

Dead tree branch twigs divide the sky
bisect the universal landscape
squirrel bodies are broken
reflectionless gray overwhelms
it dyes everything,
our skin looks like the air.

Some want to smile
moving forward, buzzing earth veins
warming on living to live.

Others are incapable,
they need to incinerate,
explode,
become the fire.